PHOTO CREDITS:

Lee Whittles, cover; Graphicon, Ltd.—pps.6,18;
Royal V. Carley—p.9; Carl Moreus—pps.10,14,22;
Gene Ruestmann—pps.13,29; Robert C. Grana—p.17;
Ken Blumberg—p.21; James Power—p.25;
Klauss Brahmst—p.26.

Amazing Grace

THE C. R. GIBSON COMPANY

NORWALK, CONNECTICUT

Amazing grace! how sweet the sound
That saved a wretch like me!

Grace comes into the soul, as the morning sun
into the world; first a dawning; then a light;
and at last the sun in his full and excellent
brightness

THOMAS ADAMS

Whatever troubles come on you, of mind, body, or
estate, from within or from without, from chance
or from intent, from friends or foes—whatever
your trouble be, though you be lonely, O children
of a heavenly Father, be not afraid!

JOHN HENRY NEWMAN

Be strong and of a good courage, fear not, nor
be afraid of them: for the Lord thy God, he it
is that doth go with thee; he will not fail thee,
nor forsake thee.

DEUTERONOMY 31:6

Raise your heart continually to God, seek His
aid, and let the foundation stone of your con-
solation be your happiness in being His. All
vexations and annoyances will be comparatively
unimportant while you know that you have such
a Friend, such a Stay, such a Refuge. May God
be ever in your heart.

St. FRANCIS DE SALES

I once was lost, but now am found,
Was blind, but now I see.

The grace of God is the good which God puts into
each concrete situation over and above all that
man can do or plan or even imagine.
HENRY N. WIEMAN

The Lord openeth the eyes of the blind: the
Lord raiseth them that are bowed down: the Lord
loveth the righteous.
PSALM 146:8

How God rejoices over a soul, which, surrounded
on all sides by suffering and misery, does that
upon earth which the angels do in heaven; namely,
loves, adores, and praises God!
GERHARD TERSTEEGEN

Be still, my soul! Thy God doth undertake
  To guide the future, as He has the past:
Thy hope, thy confidence, let nothing shake,
  All now mysterious shall be bright at last.
JANE BORTHWICK

Grant us, O Lord, we beseech Thee, always to
seek Thy kingdom and righteousness, and of
whatsoever Thou seest us to stand in need,
mercifully grant us an abundant portion.
Amen

'Twas grace that taught my heart to fear,
And grace my fears relieved;

Then shall thy light break forth as the morning,
and thine health shall spring forth speedily:
and thy righteousness shall go before thee; the
glory of the Lord shall be thy rereward.
Then shalt thou call, and the Lord shall answer;
thou shalt cry, and he shall say, Here I am . . .
ISAIAH 58:8,9

Let us therefore come boldly unto the throne of
grace, that we may obtain mercy, and find grace
to help in time of need.
HEBREWS 4:16

I sought the Lord, and afterward I knew
He moved my soul to seek him, seeking me;
It was not I that found, O Saviour true;
No, I was found of thee.
ANONYMOUS

Almighty God, who hast poured upon us the new
light of thine incarnate Word; Grant
that the same light enkindled in our hearts
may shine forth in our lives through
Jesus Christ our Lord.
Amen

How precious did that grace appear
The hour I first believed!

God is a thousand times more ready to give than
to receive.

MEISTER ECKHART

God bids us, then, by past mercies, by present
grace, by fears of coming ill, by hopes in His
goodness, earnestly, with our whole hearts, seek
Him and His righteousness, and all these things,
all ye need for soul and body, peace, comfort,
joy, the overflowing of His consolations, shall
be added over and above to you.

EDWARD BOUVERIE PUSEY

Sink into the sweet and blessed littleness, where
thou livest by grace alone. Contemplate with de-
light the holiness and goodness in God, which
thou dost not find in thyself. How lovely it is
to be nothing when God is all!

GERHARD TERSTEEGEN

Thou that hast given so much to me,
Give one thing more, a grateful heart.
Not thankful when it pleaseth me,
As if thy blessings had spare days;
But such a heart, whose pulse may be
    Thy praise.

GEORGE HERBERT

Through many dangers, toils, and snares, I have already come;

Grace is unconquerable love ... waits not for merit to call it forth, but flows out to the most guilty, is the sinner's only hope.

WILLIAM ELLERY CHANNING

But now thus saith the Lord that created thee, O Jacob, and he that formed thee, O Israel, Fear not: for I have redeemed thee, I have called thee by thy name; thou art mine.
When thou passest through the waters, I will be with thee; and through the rivers, they shall not overflow thee: when thou walkest through the fire, thou shalt not be burned, neither shall the flame kindle upon thee.
For I am the Lord thy God ...

ISAIAH 43:1-3

... the God of all grace, who hath called us unto his eternal glory by Christ Jesus, after that ye have suffered a while, make you perfect, stablish, strengthen, settle you.

I PETER 5:10

Jesus, thou friend divine,
  Our Saviour and our King,
Thy hand from every snare and foe
  Shall great deliverance bring.

TIMOTHY DWIGHT

'Tis grace hath brought me safe thus far,
And grace will lead me home.

Abandon yourself to His care and guidance, as a sheep in the care of a shepherd, and trust Him utterly. No matter though you may seem to yourself to be in the very midst of a desert, with nothing green about you, inwardly or outwardly, and may think you will have to make a long journey before you can get into the green pastures. Our Shepherd will turn that very place where you are into green pastures, for He has power to make the desert rejoice and blossom as a rose.

HANNAH WHITALL SMITH

Wherever he may guide me,
   No want shall turn me back;
My Shepherd is beside me,
   And nothing can I lack.
His wisdom ever waketh,
   His sight is never dim,—
   He knows the way he taketh,
   And I will walk with him.

ANNA L. WARING

For I the Lord thy God will hold thy right hand, saying unto thee, Fear not; I will help thee.

ISAIAH 41:13

The Lord has promised good to me, His word my hope secures;

He shall call upon me, and I will answer him: I will be with him in trouble; I will deliver him, and honour him.
With long life will I satisfy him, and shew him my salvation.

PSALM 91.15,16

Thy kingdom come, with power and grace,
  To every heart of man;
Thy peace, and joy, and righteousness
  In all our bosoms reign.

CHARLES WESLEY

If any one would tell you the shortest, surest way to all happiness and all perfection, he must tell you to make it a rule to yourself to thank and praise God for everything that happens to you. For it is certain that whatever seeming calamity happens to you, if you thank and praise God for it, you turn it into a blessing. Could you, therefore, work miracles, you could not do more for yourself than by this thankful spirit; for it heals with a word speaking, and turns all that it touches into happiness.

WILLIAM LAW

He will my shield and portion be
As long as life endures.

For the Lord God is a sun and shield: the Lord
will give grace and glory: no good thing will
he withhold from them that walk uprightly.
O Lord of hosts, blessed is the man that trusteth
in thee.

PSALM 84:11,12

The King of love my shepherd is,
   Whose goodness faileth never;
I nothing lack if I am his,
   And he is mine for ever.

HENRY WILLIAMS BAKER

Cast thy burdens upon the Lord, —hand it over,
heave it upon Him,—*and He shall sustain thee;*
shall bear both, if thou trust Him with both,
both thee and thy burden: *He shall never suffer
the righteous to be moved.*

ROBERT LEIGHTON

We have only to be patient, to pray, and to do
His will, according to our present light and
strength, and the growth of the soul will go
on. The plant grows in the mist and under clouds
as truly as under sunshine. So does the heavenly
principle within.

WILLIAM ELLERY CHANNING

Yea, when this flesh and heart shall fail,
And mortal life shall cease,

God would not have given us souls capable of
contemplating and desiring this holy eternity, if
He had not intended to bestow on us the means
of obtaining it.

St. FRANCIS DE SALES

And so through all the length of days
  Thy goodness faileth never:
Good Shepherd, may I sing thy praise
  Within thy house for ever.

HENRY WILLIAMS BAKER

He who believes in God is not careful for the
morrow, but labors joyfully and with a great
heart. "For He giveth His beloved, as in sleep."
They must work and watch, yet never be careful
or anxious, but commit all to Him, and live in
serene tranquillity; with a quiet heart, as one
who sleeps safely and quietly.

MARTIN LUTHER

Grant to me above all things that can be desired,
to rest in Thee, and in Thee to have my heart at
peace. Thou art the true peace of the heart,
Thou its only rest; out of Thee all things are
hard and restless. In this very peace, that is,
in Thee, the One Chiefest Eternal Good, I will
sleep and rest. Amen.

THOMAS À KEMPIS

I shall possess, within the veil,
A life of joy and peace.

Grace is but glory begun, and glory is but grace perfected.

JONATHAN EDWARDS

He will guide us in a sure path, though it be a rough one: yet He will be with us. He will bring us home at last. By His eye or by His voice He will guide us, if we be docile and gentle; by His staff and by His rod, if we wander or are wilful: any how, and by all means, He will bring us to His rest.

HENRY EDWARD MANNING

Knowing that he which raised up the Lord Jesus shall raise up us also by Jesus, and shall present us with you.
For all things are for your sakes, that the abundant grace might through the thanksgiving of many redound to the glory of God.

II CORINTHIANS 4:14,15

O King, O Christ, this endless grace
    To us and all men bring,
To see the vision of thy face
    In joy, O Christ, our King.

L. B. C. L. MUIRHEAD

Amazing Grace! How Sweet the Sound.

Gratitude does nothing but love God because of
the greatness of His bounty and proclaims His
goodness unceasingly . . . It will be a foretaste
of heaven to us here below, if we are able to
thank God for all His infinite goodness with
all our heart.

OTTOKAR PROHASZKA

All that is high and holy in human life meets
in that faith which is born of the unveiling of
a heaven that has always been; in that hope of
a vision of the heaven that shall be; in that
love which creates a heaven in the eternal Now.

FRIEDRICH FROEBEL

Grace and peace be multiplied unto you through
the knowledge of God, and of Jesus our Lord,
According as his divine power hath given unto us all
things . . . through the knowledge of him that hath
called us to glory and virtue:
Whereby are given unto us exceeding great and
precious promises: that by these ye might be
partakers of the divine nature . . .

II PETER 1:2-4

Amazing grace! how sweet the sound
That saved a wretch like me!
I once was lost, but now am found,
Was blind, but now I see.

'Twas grace that taught my heart to fear,
And grace my fears relieved;
How precious did that grace appear
The hour I first believed!

Through many dangers, toils, and snares,
I have already come;
'Tis grace hath brought me safe thus far,
And grace will lead me home.

The Lord has promised good to me,
His word my hope secures;
He will my shield and portion be
As long as life endures.

Yea, when this flesh and heart shall fail,
And mortal life shall cease,
I shall possess, within the veil,
A life of joy and peace.
  Amen